As She Falls,

Writing Esme Rose

As She Falls

She Rises

By Esme Rose Carrington

As She Falls, She Rises

Copyright © Esme Rose Carrington, 2020

All rights reserved. No part of this publication may be reproduced, distributed, or transmitted in any form or by any means, without the prior written permission of the publisher, except by a reviewer who may quote brief passages in a review.

The publisher apologises for any errors and would be grateful if notified of any corrections that should be incorporated in future reprints or editions of this book.

First paper back edition January 2020 Book designed by Esme Rose Carrington

ISBN: 9798739724854 **Imprint**: Independently published through kindle direct publishing.

For my soul family

As She Falls, She Rises

Feel the tick tock drop

look into the sky

where is time?

but an illusion in your mind

take it all off

undress your skin bare

until all that is left

is

your circling breath.

Close your eyes

breathe a deep breath into your belly

feel your lungs fill up with air

as you exhale

empty everything out

make this longer than your inhale

take a moment

or two

to ground yourself into this moment through conscious breathing

Welcome to As She Falls She Rises

This book holds a compilation of the poetry I wrote throughout 2020, this books creation has served as medicine to me and it is my pure intention that it will be medicinal for you too.

As She Falls She Rises intends to assist you through whatever weather you may be growing through, to remind you that you are never alone, to guide you, to hold you, to see you, to celebrate you, to honour you, to be an open and transparent portal of truth that brings you back to who you really are time and time again.

Every poem within has been inspired by my walk with life so far, capturing the ups the downs and everything inbetween, through writing I have learnt to welcome every lick of colour that being human paints. The feathers that decorate this book have held me through my inner world of turbulence, now it is time for them to hold you, every time you find feathers dancing on the pages ask them a question, see them as angels appearing as ink.

Listen to your body as you receive your own wisdom.

You are a miracle in form, you are spirit observing life, consciousness with your own unique mind, as human beings we attach to experiences and somewhere along the way we forget that it is not life happening to us, but us witnessing the unravelling of our life, there is always a silent observer and that observer is who you really are, no god outside of you, no god hidden within the crevices of this planet, just you pretending you are everything and anything but that which you seek, each soul you cross paths with is a reflection of you, when you peer into anothers eyes you're looking into their soul.

The identity that you've shaped yourself into will likely create an opinion about all of this,

however the truth is found in what you feel.

This is the journey we seek, right here wherever you are with life planted beneath your feet,
we are lovingly walking one another back to the home within.

is planted in the summer of 2018, I was on a train for
travelling from Exeter to the Lake District, I spent the
tying my insides out, re-writing who I was and
for myself for the first time. I noticed a fleeting thought and a
whispering feeling of inspiration to one day create my own book of poetry, not knowing how or when or why, but trusting in the birthing of the unknown. The seed began growing its roots in autumn of 2019, I was on another train travelling through Sweden chasing lakes eagerly when the name of this book announced itself to me, I pulled out my notebook ready to receive and spill the contents within... now addicted to the mystery, from here onwards I began to trust in the unseen, the earth, the universe, the feathers, the train journeys. I began to trust *everything* and this is how I learnt to trust myself. The stem first sprouted in January 2020 when I published the first edition of this book, premature she was, it didn't feel right so I began editing again only to continue rushing her growth under the pressure and expectation of perfection that I had put on myself, I stopped sharing and selling the second edition of this book in spring of 2020 to focus more on my relationship with *self*, I began painting again and kept my words very close to home allowing myself to fully receive what I was writing, time trickled by as it always does and my intuition was nudging me to begin again, so I did. The entire contents of As She Falls She Rises transformed much like a catapillar going through metamorphosis. I slowly and steadily spent spring, summer, autumn and winter of 2020 working closely with this books unravelling, I began shaping my poems in a different way allowing for my heart to simply show me the way, I added poems, I changed poems, I deleted poems, I laughed, I cried, I realised I was not learning how to create a book but I was learning how to create myself. Her leaves were flourishing and her petals preparing to bloom, so I published the third editon in February of 2021, trusting the wings of this book to travel across Earth and land into the palms of those who were meant to receive her in her third form. As She Falls She Rises has become an extension of me, as I change she does too, so here I find myself sipping on my rooibos tea accompanied by the unpredictable english weather on the 5th May 2021, making adjustments within and without, guided by something greater than me, trusting in something I can't see, following the feeling of truth as I continuously come home to more of me. As She Falls She Rises has been the therapy I always needed, her petals now strong enough to hold pearls. This book has bloomed, she is a flower, open, soft, gentle, free, her nectar sweet and ready to be received by *all of you.*

Love exists in others, but it first must exist in oneself.

Creator being
come home to your ethereal silk
as you emerge from your chrysalis
it is time to rise
with your wings held high
connect to the roots of this earthly realm

you are remembering who *you* are

let the unravelling of your life unfold
in its own chosen delight
envision your *being*
being held in emerald light

trust where your soles are

one step in front of the other.

Oh ocean waves you cleanse away
what has never been named
ocean waves you are the days
I rest within

dearest lungs of the earth
I surrender to you
take me slowly into your palms as I deliver what is
asking to be seen

"why me" I may plead
yet no answer is neccessary to be received

talking in riddles giving space for the mind to
unwind
camaflaged by the night

no escaping from the light that intends to
breathe.

Love is true and it is you

do not be afraid of being you

yes you are not for everyone

but everyone is not for you.

As She Falls, She Rises

One can not wake someone else up, nor can we force a different lens onto someone who believes what they see, but through offering contrasting insight it is an invitation to delve deeper within, and in this scuba diving of sorts we come to understand we're all walking our own maze, without realising it is illusory, there is no maze, nor is there a key, it is a distorted belief to think you are not already free. The mind will trip you up and trick you, convincing you of the stories you perceive running through your mind, so ask yourself why must you hide from really seeing the miracle it is that you can even breathe, that you are even alive, why are we collectively playing hide and seek from the god we think we are not, when did we get mixed up and begin to believe the minds rambling speech, when did love and peace stop being what we preach, why are we weak for not believing what we see, when did our innate wisdom become suppressed, when did talking about individual truth and vibration become taboo or out of interest?

I invite you to look up to the moon, the sun, the stars, the clouds, not for what you call a second, but for a moment in this now, let the infinite sky hold your gaze and as you are holding this gaze breathe in slowly, feel the rise and fall, can you allow yourself to remember the deep, true miracle that you are?

Love is at your fingertips
be bold in choosing to exist with it.

I find myself in moments of seraphic bliss
diving into euphoria
absorbing all that surrounds me as I float in pure stillness
I witness the creation of beautiful memories slipping
through my fingertips

Breathing in tune with the drum in my chest
lightening cracks through the sky
nature reminds me to embrace the tide
thunder echoes frantically in my mind
but the storm always passes and
alchemizes into light

in every fall

I rise.

You belong exactly as you are from this moment to the next
you are a breath of fresh air
you owe it to yourself to *breathe in* your own love

baby steps now
remember the race only exists in your mind.

Look around
observe the glorious life surrounding you
create dreams and know they are never too big.

Life is an emotional journey that you are able to
flow with
sometimes it may feel stormy
and as though the hurricane will never pass
but it always does
you will find yourself afloat

Begin to believe that you are able to live life fully
then embrace and observe every heart beat
for *it is* beating for you

breathing is medicine
trust your breath

you truly are your own healer.

You are whole as you are
every broken piece you've created along the way
is still within you
on a journey of its own individual healing

your cracks will form together
in a way more beautiful than you can imagine.

Feeling soft flows of the oceans ripple
colliding through me and dancing with my soul

oh to feel so deeply has never been a curse
but it is a gift
to live
so fluently in tune with
every passing emotion
no more controlling the motion
in which vibration is experienced across the nation
love too strong to be held down
light too bright to be diminished now.

All is welcome here
for all we know is this
a manifestation of bliss
we must remember we are the witness
feeding off of the seeds of an illusory authority

too fogged in amnesia to see
clearly

we are the fragmented pieces that the riches
deem to play with

to awaken from this trick is to observe ones own
delusional misfit

freedom is no figure of speech, nor out of reach,
so let us preach

the truth
of who we really are.

Dripping into notes of river flowing music
breathing inside the moment whilst my mind tries to escape

come back

I whisper to myself softly as I begin to dance in navy smoke.

You are exactly where you are supposed to be and
you're doing just fine

keep on breathing into you

love yourself the way you deserve to be loved.

Remember kindness is free and it's also the greatest gift
smile at strangers and dance with your shadow.

You are already perfect as you are.

As She Falls, She Rises

Emptying her pain into something she can understand
words float around

her hands are too weak to write

a deep red melts into a sunset of rich colour
the sky willingly carries echoes of her emotions   away

the raw beauty of the sky softly reminds her that she too
can start again as often as she needs.

Held so lovingly within natures arms
breathing a little deeper
feeling the drum of her beat
she melts
into
the
breeze.

We choose the colours in which we see life through
we are not limited to one weather
sometimes it may feel as though we experience several seasons
within just a day
so surrender to the rain
the grey clouds
the rainbows
the sun
the snow
the blizzards
the hail
surrender to the ray of weather that curls in your mind
the more you try to control your emotions
the more they'll roar

let what is passing be felt

slow down there is no rush now

the snow will melt.

Dreams of cotton
waiting to see my life unfold
emptying myelf into the current of every now
becoming one within the warm rain
dancing in showers feeling safe within my body
I am strong in every place I have been weak.
Scars clothe my skin and I let the feathered lines
control my mind causing me to hide the
gleaming light that I knew was always inside
some would say it was inside my smile and
perhaps it was only I who was hiding from the light.

your soul is in your eyes

my dear friend do not be afraid of the light
know that every breath you take is a breath of
commitment to your life. I stand with inner peace,
extending my creative mind into all that surrounds me
strokes of paint, flickers of fire, droplets of rain
singing in candle light

returning to your skin is one of the most beautiful things.

— 'Your soul is in your eyes' words spoken from
a nurse who understood the language of energy.

Blessed to be breathing

life curls so much you may get caught up and tied up
barely being able to move so you give up moving
and just
stay
stuck...
break the cycle
turn into fire and burn through
the ropes holding you so tightly

do not become a slave to society
break through old roots and grow new ones

bloom.

His hands are maps for her fingertips to dance within
golden warmth melts from his palms into hers
their fingertips dance in the vibration of love
clasping together woven secrets of how they always
knew they were supposed to be one.

Beautifully held within her quiet enclosed world
she began letting go of everything that no longer served
tip-toeing with confidence into the freshly laid soil
she began flying within the maps his palms helped her paint
eventually guiding herself back to her own heart beat

discovering her home has always been within.

Pearled navy smoke finds me painting
clouds inbetween the gaps of my body
the harsh wind gathers the shadowed parts of me
setting them free
as I witness myself detaching from my past pain I
feel my insides swirling and twirling in celebration
as if I am quilted in silk.

Pain is never permanent, self destruction brings self discovery
self remembrance

you are going to be okay.

Serenity joins me within these feathered oceans
dipping into peace
as water purifies my soul
and cleanses my mind
my wings were created
in the white roaring feathers of the sea
I am as devoted to honouring myself
as the moon is committed to controlling the tide
we are one
there is no seperation
only desperation
for unity
and for
love.

Drop in,

dive in

to the crevices of your skin, the   shadows   within,

allow your love to ripple through,
giving   *space*   for your soul to move.

 Don't underestimate the power of you.

As She Falls, She Rises

We have been programmed to suppress and distract ourselves from the
true gift of our human experience, slowly slipping further away from the truth,
fear has been heavily induced,
tricking us into amnesia,
destroying our roots;
drowning ourselves in fear because that seems easier then stepping
into the true authentic you,
yet things are changing,
there is a choice, a choice to swim in tune with the tide of this crumbling matrix,
or a choice to break free,
breathing into love

surrendering to the stream.

You are not here by chance, your human existence is no accident,
you have been perfectly designed for the life you are courageously living,

being human isn't always easy.

Captivated by colours unpainted
fresh linen to carress my bones
snow carpets the floor
grass peeks through
playing peek a boo with winter
the heavens open
lilacs and you
enticed by the wings of these singing birds
they live so free up there

I exhale and clarity arises
a clear channel for the divine to spiral through

I remember my first love
I looked her in the mirror once
and decided to stay twice

I am growing fearlessly into the unknown
I find myself latching on to every passing moment
ensuring I don't miss any of it

For a long time I didn't know life could feel so soft

I am cocooned in my own skin
and
welcomed home by my own love.

Creating shapes dancing to candle light
harmonies of offbeat humming echoes through these
tapestry walls

Collapsing into the depths of my being discovering I
am already whole exactly as I am.

Take down the mask that you've gotten so used to hiding behind

unfold your wings

watch yourself evolve into who you know you are.

As She Falls, She Rises

No one can deny you of your own lived experience
or the wisdom you gained through it
only *you* know your truth
and it is not your job to convince others of your inner knowing
but it is your choice to share your lived wisdom
without attachment to who may listen
for those who are willing to receive will naturally be by your side energetically
with their hearts wide open
ears listening
clinging on
to the medicine your soul speaks for it will remind them of their own
spirits tone
bringing them back into presence of where the language of the divine source is spoken
so may you softly offer your contrasting insight on what is felt before it is written
into the depths of the beings who have been dampened and distanced
from their own intuition
we are here to gently remind one another that we are all one family
the same species
there is no need for a loveless war
we must balance the feminine and masculine energy
creatively nurturing one another
regardless of where we are planted upon the map of earth
no complexion can seperate
we are here to simply rise
into our truest expression of medicine
healing men and healing women

opening the curtain
beckoning for the insanity of the mind to look inside

what a ride

it is

to be alive.

Life is a happening
are your eyes opened or closed?

As She Falls, She Rises

The last licks of summer melt into crimson
rays of old green days
auburn fire blankets the floor
awaiting the crunching galore of autumn
to somersault into bitterly crisp air
larva beneath the feet
turns into broken golden leaves
trees fall bare
the smell of pine cones swirl in the air
blue skies so clear you know winter is near
feeling it all, much like the rain fall
I reclaim myself here
standing strong in these shivering bones
I choose to rise consciously
I commit to loving unconditionally
full moon, a rose in bloom
midnight air shakes me as I attempt to sleep
under the same blanket of stars that saved me.

I distructed and dismantled myself until fragments
of who I had once been began decaying and
disintegrating into an abyss wallowing beneath me,

once I started to breathe softly again
I enabled myself to choose how I was going to continue living
I had to accept that the life I was living
was of an emotional one
and I was either all in or all out,

I no longer wanted to feel heavy every time my heart beat

instead I wanted to feel
euphoria respect and exhilaration
for the vessel I was existing in
regardless of if I felt like I belonged in it or not.

- Life is a canvas, everyday you have the
choice to create what this canvas will look like, you are
the decider of the colours and how you will use them. Perhaps you
can use this in a metaphoric way and apply this to
emotions, you'll see you have a choice in how to react to every
emotion you feel, whether to let it pass through or whether to
suppress it, just like the paints you can decide which colours
to paint your days with.
I observe/feelings as water, understanding that the water will
pass at whichever speed it is intended too.
Be aware of what is passing through but understand whatever

you may be feeling does not and will never define you,
you are not the depression that drums in your mind and
echoes through your body, nor are you the anxiety that leaves
you shaking and aching.
You are wonderful.

Choose a new canvas as many times as you need to,
paint your days in a way that makes you show up for you.

Don't punish yourself for being human.

Do you realise how much courage it takes to be so
unapologetically you?
You are a warrior
you are incredible
your worth is not defined by anything external.

When the pain is too thick in your lungs
that you can no longer breathe
hold on to your heart
and let it lead you home

you will get through this day
allow for your soul to show you the way.

You deserve
honesty
truth
love
and devotion

don't settle for anything less.

You are love
you are light
you are all things gloriously radiant in golden sunshine
you are the rivers and oceans
the rolling hills
and the climbing mountains
you are life itself

do you see how powerful that is?

You are life itself.

-Repeat this over and over until you start to feel your own belonging.

Clouds come and go, but the sun always finds a way through,
the sun is you, you can always find a way through.

Quilted in love

devoted to the rhythm of me
sharing my authenticity

born again to my souls purpose
my heart is blessed to be free

Create what your soul intends
for you to see
follow those intuitive whispers
trust them and believe.

Never accept a love that doesn't spill as ocean deep as yours does again.

Loving yourself is the bravest thing you can do
release any false perception of love
rebel fearlessly in loving you

love yourself the same way you desire to be loved by another.

Live every day as if it is your last day on earth
living as a human being,
you don't need to do anything extraordinary
rather allow the day to unfold naturally and
treat every passing moment with tender presence
find the sacred essence within each pulse you beat
slow down
savor every passing breath
this is where you will find your feet
that have always been beneath
guiding you
showing you
teaching you

 remember to *just* be.

Unwinding fear

untangling what once was a mind bedded with weeds

soil is fresh

roots can breathe

humanity is beginning to see
clearly.

-We are walking through a movie on replay that we label as life, we fit into our identitys and play the character we've shaped ourselves into, we attach to experiences and define ourselves by them, we call truth conspiracy theories and consume the lies we're hand fed, then complain about the 'mess' it seems we're in, yet it's all an illusion that society doesn't want you to see, so will you stop being the sheep and re-evaluate what it is that you truly believe.

You reminded me of the sea
the way you rolled back and forth into my heart
the roughness of your waves were enough to drown me

I wanted to be a collected sea shell,
not a grain of sand left in your bed.

- I bathed in a negative relationship unaware of the damage I
was doing to myself, I had detached myself from who I knew
I was, I am grateful for all of the experiences I have had for
they have led me to this now, sharing this message, hoping to
catch whoever needs to be caught, see this message as a sign
perhaps to step away from something that is no longer
positively serving you, know it's okay to walk away.
It is brave and courageous to put yourself first.
Everything is always working out for you.

As She Falls, She Rises

Oh the sweet melody you are,

I see you, not with my eyes,
    but with my soul,

I hear you, not with my ears,
    but with my heart.

Respect your love in the form of a home,
nurture and care for all of the hidden rooms,
create a sanctuary for your love to grow and expand.

Don't be afraid of loving yourself.

- There was a time when I was physically
destructing myself, I ached to climb out of this
vessel and return into the cosmos, I never thought a
time would come when I could look at myself and
really see me through the eyes of love, or acceptance.
It has been a journey of some sort to get to where
I am right now, a lot of tears, a lot of pain, a lot of rainy
days, but here I remain.

I'll be honest with you, there are still some moments
when I feel detached from who I am, I look in the
mirror searching for 'me', only to remember all of this is me,
the searching, the seeking, the finding,
it is the I playing with the divine, hide and seek if you like.
Loving yourself is a process, it doesn't happen
instantly, it is an ever growing journey of choosing
yourself over and over again, but it gets easier and
there will come a day when you will see that all of
the times you danced with the rain were worth the
internal pain.
Let your love cascade over you, begin
right now by telling yourself *I love you.*

As She Falls, She Rises

Words fall into tears,
creating storms as I stumble trying to create
something beautiful out of this humiliating pain,
years have floated by,
yet your fingertips are still engraved on my skin,
faces blur into no one,
I'm left with images of a torturous time that I can't
even recall.

- Through the pain that still echoes throughout my mind and
shivers through my body I find solidity within my own tears
and growth with every crippling flashback.
Yes I've been hurt and my body has been
misused, but I am no longer a victim, I am bold and new,
I no longer define myself as another humans prey,
I take ownership of everything I am and I hope you can too.

It's as if I'm caught in a tide,
I keep getting pulled back in
then dragged across the shore,
neither one pretty both leaving me sore.

I say the ocean feels like home,
but perhaps that's because of the uncertainty that follows,
you never know if you're going to drown in the storm
or glisten in the sun.

-For so long I had gotten so used to fighting the current in which I was swimming upstream in, I got battered and bruised loosing all control, but in this process I realised I was trying to shape water rather then just let it be and let it flow.

Flowing is the key, you have to let the currents flow as fast or as slow as they come, without judgment, but with grace. When I'm feeling heavy and clogged up, I lay down flat on the floor and breathe, lying down surrendering and connecting back to your breath will help you assist the clearing of the emotions through your body.

Emotion- E motion = energy in motion

I can't shape this feeling into words,
floating through clouds,
blinded by the fog,
gasping for comfort to soothe me again,
never have I ever felt so blue.

- Be in the colours that surround you, dive into your mind.

Figure out where the fog is trying to form a cloud
and acknowledge whatever emotion it is.
Allow it to be felt, let your sunshine mind create gaps in
the clouds where blue seeps into your existence,
where you feel gently held again within the warmth of your heart,

eventually you'll find yourself back in the moment you were always in.

You are still healing and that's okay.

You are healing and that's a miracle.

Go through life with an outlook that it's on fire
burn gloriously into the flames
let the world see you.

Our hearts beat in tune
we are our own rhythm,
balencing ourselves upon the waves of this unfolding life

hold me closer

I can feel more than your skin
unfold yourself into my love and feel the freedom
that runs through
you.

As the leaves turn red,
she turns golden,
falling into a new home of clarity.

Emotions flow as if they are a river caught in a riptide
become one with the water
trickle over rocks
get caught up with the twigs

embrace the unknown
let go
flow with the river
dance with the storm

bask in the sun
be gentle with you

life is a dance and you are the composer of the
tune you dance too.

Slipping under my bed sheets as I whisper prayers
of gratitude for another day in Eden,

diving in,
fully surrendering,
believing in the rhythmic flow as I breathe in tune
with the drum in my chest,

fully immersed within each breath,

gripping on to the pulse of life,
slipping in further to this human vessel,
embodying the highest version of myself,
being the light I always intended to be,

I see you
as you see me,
open,
honest,
raw and free.

there is no one else like you.

Watching myself from afar
telling my younger self secrets of how my life is shaped now
I tell her all is well and we're breathing in harmony.

Silence is the teacher
Spirit is the messenger
You are the observer

Do not be afraid of the seasons
watch them as you become them
return to natures pace
remember there is no race.

In the darkness of your days,
search for the flickering light,
honour yourself in gentle pulsations of love,

nourish your body with everything you
wholesomely deserve.

Earth is Eden,
you are an extension of the energy that creates entire galaxies,
living in human form creating your reality through your thoughts.

You are more than this physical body,
you are a multidimensional being.

Words are falling,
there is a rhythm in my mind,
soft pitter-pattering of rain drops
flow through effortlessly,
I begin creating a waterfall of movements,
feeling each ripple of magic cleansing my soul,
I twirl and spin in tune with the goddess within,
life is succulent,
I cling on to every moment ensuring I am fully
present in every now,

I belong,
I belong,
I belong.

-I repeat these words *I belong* to myself as often as I
need to, they are soft but powerful. If you feel yourself
drifting away from yourself, try bringing yourself back to
this moment with these words.

Write them down, shout them out,
do whatever you need to, to remember you belong
exactly as you are, wherever you are, right here, right now.

Choosing to live whilst lying limp in a hospital bed
body carressed with tubes
beeping of the machines echoing frantically through empty walls
a few breaths away from collapsing into death
I emptied myself onto the concrete of the devils doorstep
surrendering myself to what I had been waiting for
only
it was not the devils doorstep that I emptied myself on to
but it was a heaven
held by angelic feathers
every inch of my skin kissed by loving silk

Angels began appearing from the depths of a screen
pulling me into a hallucinated dream
comforted by the strokes of a soft breeze
long grass enveloping me
sweet humming of birds showing me

Gaia calling me
cradling me
piecing me
back together.

Saved by my own inner grace.

Weightless against the pull of this shift
immersed within the movement of these new roots

taking apart the layers of human programming

our souls are no longer buried deep within

smiles are gestures of love
life is changing.

Loving yourself is an art
you get to choose the colours *you* paint yourself with
so choose the ones *you* love the most.

-Mine was black for a while, until I discovered the colours that even a rainbow doesn't know.

There's always a way to get through the day
 breathe deeply press your palm onto your heart

feel your pulse
follow it home.

You can never be too kind,
the world can only be seen as too cruel,

stay humble and remain sharing your divinity,
you are igniting the light in others.

Stand tall
uniquely free yourself and cloak your

dermis in the ocean silk
welcome in your fears and heal them through your

own compassion
invite tears and be thankful for when they fall

You are incredibly brave and so powerful by simply being you.

I've been becoming some sort of spiritual
nophologist
observing so many angels flying high
camouflaging themselves as nimbus clouds
boldly thriving above clear as the day

yet it's our choice to look up
our choice to see through what we can see
our choice to recognise the power in being
fully alive and fluently free

fully you and fully me

Step out of the controlled game

step in
to you.

My being is ever growing through every breath
energy of my soul is dancing
amongst the moonlight of the jungle
in which my dreams rest in
lapping water welcomes me home

dancing in sand I know I belong.

Angelic voices dripping into my awareness
making a home in the crevices of my skin
burning slowly into flickering candles
moving in slow motion
spilling across a canvas
creating something magical
defining art with the drips of my mind
every golden soul crumbling into one
melting into a painting
radiating across the universe

We are all fragments of stars.

Curve your body into patterns of the solar system
flow in the direction of unity
move your body
don't try to fit yourself into boxes

unlock the cage you *feel* yourself in
society is a game that you don't have to play

you know who you are, come back to you

allow your roots to grow untamed and free,

you can't go too far wrong being wholesomely yourself.

Birds

here I float amongst the uncertainty of what today will bring
birds sing sweetly as I search for the courage to
awaken from this hibernation
I find
myself lost again within the depths of my mind

then within the birds gracious song clarity arises

open to what I'll find

I begin to open my wings too.

The entirety of her heart overflows with love
she can not contain this felicity
to be alive is precious
to feel alive is a gift she will never again take for granted
she loves herself so fiercely for diving so deeply
into everything she discovered herself to be
Content within each wave she is carried by
in flow with the unpredictable currents of life

We never experience anything we are not ready for.

Sweet honey do not waste your dear time
trying to please people who will never truly
be pleased.

Re-adjust your focus to you,
how can you please yourself today, what can you do for you?
Everything is vibrational, we all hold our own frequency,
sometimes we resonate with others sometimes we don't, there
is no need to dive into this or over complicate this, simply allow it to be.
Compare this analogy to food, there are some foods that you
love, some foods that you hate and some that are okay, you
don't try to force yourself to eat the food you don't like, so
don't force yourself into being a certain way just for the sake
of someone else, trust your taste-buds, trust your resonance.

Get lost in the ocean as it spills across the shore
soak in the sound of the birds
bathe in the sun
dive into peace

Settle into who you know yourself to be
float amongst the bliss of being
simply.

When you can begin to see life with love,
you'll find yourself breathing *in* peace.

Your pain will turn into beauty.

Stumbling across words trying to form something as beautiful as you.

Love remains within.

These words are for you,

everything you feel is necessary,
in every moment your heart beats try
and match the rhythm and stay present
with that subtle drum,
when you can learn to quieten the stream
of thoughts trickling through your mind
you'll allow a stream of guidance to spill
through instead, listen to the murmurs,
your intuition is your truth.

Your authenticity *is* your gift

The gift you think you must search for *is* nestled within your rib cage, it *is* the drum that pulses you through the day

the breath that guides you time and time again

your gift *is* your truth

is   your   humble   presence   upon   this   Earth

walking this world.

The cosmo of today envelopes me in a state of ecstacy,
draw me in colour, I'll be more than the grey, allow me to show you the
way the sky turns into a display of enticing rays when you peel back the
layers of everything that defines you,
stripped back to your core,
who are you?

Do you wake up every day feeling joy within the birds song,
or crumble under your duvet as the distracted thoughts kick in,
you are here on purpose, with intent, there is so much strength within you,
let the whispers unravel,
you've got your very own guidance system,

heal yourself with your own medicine.

- I'll be honest, there are still some days that getting out of bed feels more like a
chore than a celebration, but on those days I take things slow, I whisper loving words
to myself and be gentle with my body as she feels as intensely as she does. There is
nothing wrong with what you feel, it is remembering this that will ease the
attachment to thinking your feelings aren't worthy of being felt *fully*.

Smiles gleam across our face merging into one contagious race
bold in energy as we emanate love as a remedy
like hate is the enemy
running from a melody
to close to chase the recipe
can't compare the complexity

of love

every moment a grand epiphany of witnessing the miracle that is

all of this

here we are
listening to the bliss
voice of angels
moving with the groove

easing into the moment as the car continues running
kestrels swoop in with stillness to remind us of the natural
perfection of life's reflection,

here for this
again and again

I am here for

this.

When you open yourself up you are opening yourself up to
love and love can only flow in the spaces it is meant to,
so trust
in where you find yourself here,

no matter the amount of times you attempt to close the door
of what always wants to be open,
love can not be contained, love can not be handled, love can
not be shaped, love can not be played,

love is only one energetic frequency travelling through the
constellations above you and me, forever flowing,
intertwining,
weaving in and out of the web of life.

You will know you have found the one when you are looking
into the portals of your own eyes and you realise it is your
reflection that has been the one that you've always been afraid
to see,
walking through all these different lives until you come back
to your *own true self*,

let love in the whispers say, let love in the whispers call,
let love in the whispers plead.

Let love in to all of your days,
the blue the grey, the drizzling rain, the golden rays,

let love in they say.

As She Falls, She Rises

Her scars began growing flowers in a way that she could
never have imagined,
petals cloaked her skin as if she was in a cocoon of silk,
raw purple lines that reminded her of torturous
times transformed into white strokes with the
resemblance of feathers.
Anger for what she had inflicted upon herself
began making its disappearance
tears   no   longer   fell   with   shame
instead they trickled love down her cheeks as she
forgave herself for everything she believed made her weak.

Strength breathed through her as she carried
herself out of the pain, rising after yet another fall.

Let go of your grip,
you don't have to hold on so tight,
encourage the cage doors to open as if there is a
flood gate inside of you,
release whatever is holding it so firmly shut
flow with the current,
try not to dwell so much on the speed at which
you are being carried by water
rather surrender into the movement of your soul
as you set your true self free from anything and
everything that has been holding you down,
let the current guide you.

Be rebellious in loving yourself,
rebel against anything that has attempted to
contain you, you are power,
take back what is already yours.

As She Falls, She Rises

Surrounded by the warmest love
engulfed in the sweetest arms
purring echoes through the rooms
I've been watered daily, nurtured and cared for
but still depression creeps up like a dark tree growing
its roots in all the places there should be flowers,
the roots crack through the surface
breaking anything ready to bloom,
I embrace the crumbling despair that I find myself in,
completely oblivious to the fact that I am in full control
of where my thoughts are focused,
living in a repetitive cycle until I pull enough courage to
make the momentum stop,
trying to find the light whilst in the dark again.

As She Falls, She Rises

Choose yourself without the need of an explanation,

trust the language that spills and ripples within,

trust the pulse pulse pulse, grow with the ebbs and flows,

flower with the poppies and melt with the coming snow,

be wild and untamed,

the free orchard will bloom as you orchestrate the way,

light moves through

you.

You get everything you ask for, just not in the way your ego expects to see, the seeds you sow grow,

this is you creating your reality,

live openly, let what arises to simply just be,

don't be brainwashed by the minds religiously living in this society,

but question what the media feeds,

mind control, watch your scroll,

look at the sky not the status quo.

Peace cradles me,
strength clothes me,

love holds me, the moon guides me.

You heal people who will never even know your name.

We change, we grow,
we laugh, we cry,
effortlessly blooming every second of every day,
life isn't supposed to feel as though we are wading upstream,
release any and all resistance.
Understand life can feel good
without having to work hard to achieve that feel good state,
feeling content is our natural state of being,
bring yourself back to this consciously,

you can do this through movement and breath.

You're going to be okay.

To the grey sky that's growing into a soft blue,
welcome to winter, your glow lifts my soul,
your warm whites have a rosey echo making me feel
held in a weightless touch,
waking up softly surrounded by these walls trickling
with tapestries, oh how delicate colours are,
breathing them in as I exhale my dreams.

My love for you has settled
yet in this settlement
I am free.

Words spill from her mind as if they are water,
flowing elegantly and fluently through her body
and to her soul,
gently rising into the fullness of who she has always
known herself to be,
you see she knew her wings had been a little
damaged,
but it took her a while to see that her own love
could heal them.

Love can heal all when you let it.

-Everything is always happening with a divine reason the art of
understanding this is seeing everything as a lesson and a blessing,
I've shown myself how far my love can go by simply giving it to
this human vessel,
my heart is soft and full, my skin is beautiful and full of stories,
my life is necessary,
as is yours. I keep on writing because I know someone will read this and
it will speak to them the way poems do with me,
you are enough exactly as you are,
there is no rush, no race, no game to chase or rules to play.

As She Falls, She Rises

As the heavy pour of rain nourishes the rolling hills surrounding me
I discover that we are all one
plunging into the love that seeps through the cracks of nature
we are the ivy that grows effortlessly
flowing in no given direction but our own
sharing warmth to every being that's been cold for too long
share your light
you ignite the flame in others by keeping your fire burning.

-What happened to skipping through meadows, swinging on swings and surrendering to the rain but choosing to dance in it? We may encounter some storms in our lives, and perhaps we'll find ourselves tangled up feeling lost in a thunderstorm, but we must remember that during these times of seemingly never ending darkness we do find a light, I'm not talking about a literal light bulb, but the light that is within you,

that is your soul.

Allow yourself to heal.

These sleepless nights are falling into place
I wake when the first bird lets out the quietest hum,
nature is whispering but I hear her so clearly,
my mind is awake, rivers are flowing,

flooding with creativity, too awake to sleep.

Be kind to everything that breathes the same air as you.

Kindness is free.

Paradigms are crumbling and the new matrix is *love*.

As She Falls, She Rises

Truth is leaking into the crevices of humanity
woke in a society that wants to keep you asleep
I'm done holding my tongue, hiding behind a mask,
I gift myself to the mess
I live my life in blue, I am here for you.
Maybe I appear as eccentrically crazy,
but I will remind those that they are living by unconscious programming,
all a facade to keep the truth away, shying away from what we are facing,
messages in pyramids, we talk in numbers,
the universe is you as it is me,
observing this humanity,   no more bullshit,
I'm done with being small in this.
The world needs you as you, not a fake because you're afraid of who might see,
who might leave,
do it for the collective consciousness,
things are changing, wear your heart on your sleeve,
let your eyes bleed
truth of your soul into every being that you meet
let it all be seen.
Give it up here, the biting your lip when you know you want to speak,
the tensing in your stomach because the anxiety's rippling in,
the holding your breath because you're afraid to let it seep into the   spaces
beneath your feet
give it up here, it's not yours to hold, it's yours to release
to love   to set free   let yourself be seen.

Dear you've got to give it up, all this pretending you're everything you
know deep down you're not.

Glistening in love
I ache for you sweet honey
melting into you
shaping our bodies into one
carressed with only the kindest warmth.

Talk about how you feel in the depths of your precious heart,
your heart is a pearl and it should be handled with feathers.

Watching clouds travel across what I perceive to
be the sky
my mind has been calm and quiet

I observe my mind as I navigate through time
yet time is ever lasting if you remain in presence

life moving
pulse looping

returning to the tempo of nature

trees whisper
secrets deliver unseen shivers
blues glimmer
what is no longer serving thee is appearing thinner
release into this winter
your seasons are sacred initiations
you are constantly moving through
a transformation of who you intended to be
in this incarnation.

You are your own home,
you have nothing to be afraid of.

What you perceive as your external reality is a
reflection of what's going on internally,
soften the pressure in your mind and do
something that enables you to loosen your grip

on whatever you are choosing to hold on to,

it is safe to let go.

Close your eyes
dream of something that soothes your soul
but makes you dance
you are free to be wholesomely yourself
flowers grow in all the places pain has ever been
rain may fall but this isn't something to be afraid of
try and unfold yourself and see passing showers as
a blessing
then you will see that everything you experience is a
lesson
blooming with grace
you'll learn to adjust to the weather of your own mind,

be gentle with your seasons.

As She Falls, She Rises

...pression shaking in the corner of my mind,
...thered in a thick fog of anxiety, giving me seemingly
no choice but to nestle into the moulded darkness until I
broke through and reclaimed myself.

The thing about being human is we must learn to hold
acceptance for whatever emotion our bodies are
experiencing, understanding that the pitch black we can find ourselves
suffocating in doesn't belong to us,

it does not have the power to be our identity, even during
the times we feel as though it is all that we are.

Darkness will not stay dark,
light will seep through just as it does through blinds.

The light within us is always there, there may be some days
when we lose touch with how to ignite the flame and in
these moments we must remember to
look above to find stars.

Paint empties itself upon her flesh,
filling in the gaps of where her mind lost control,
reminding her the white strokes feathering
through her veins are droplets of art that
caress her body in a painting,

labeled as scars, but truly they are warrior lines marking
her strength.

There she stood, wide eyed as she peered into her dermis,
tracing the lines that hold memories within,

as she looked closer, she slipped in,
making a home in all of the crevices of her skin,

she was art, the type that makes you stop and breathe,
the kind that reminds you of the potency of your
own divine beat,

 She knew she was free.

You can't help someone who doesn't want to be helped, it's like trying to set water on fire,
you'll disintegrate into them letting your own flame burn out.

-Don't give up your time that is dear to you in order to try and keep someone else afloat, you are here to be present with your soul, let everything else fall into place as you focus on

your own healing,
when you can align with yourself, the energy you will then transmit to others will naturally guide them to their own medicine

As She Falls, She Rises

Open your mind as you lift your arms

release the weight you've been carrying on your shoulders

allow yourself to feel your wings

free as a bird you are.

You help others find their light through
offering your own,

don't hold yourself back from gifting your own
unique lived wisdom.

As She Falls, She Rises

Wings begin to pierce through her skin
she is determined to soar beyond heights that humans can not measure,
shape shifting into light
feathers dance in mid air as gusts of wind swoop in to gather the magic that intends to be shared
shadows float below
evaporating into the whispering clouds.

As She Falls, She Rises

She despised herself for what she had inflicted upon a
body she didn't recognise as her own
avoiding mirrors so she didn't have to witness the wreck
she created
covering her scars in art
attempting to distract herself of the times she could   barely move

not knowing the peace that she would one day breathe

until she began staring deeper
into her own existence
figuring out who she was staring back at her.

-I didn't know love could be so soft,

until I began loving myself.

Within the cracks of a speckled light,
she began breaking through the darkness that
she carved herself into.

Inspire yourself to be the person you know you are.

Life is big and brilliant, allow yourself to see this, feel this.

As She Falls, She Rises

Angels came slowly,
piecing her back together, wiping her tears,
comforting her screams, guiding her through the

darkness as she rose into light,

gentle whispers from within her soul lead her to
discovering the truth of why she stayed alive after all.

Angels stayed within her soul and nestled themselves

in the parts of her that she couldn't quite reach,
soothing themselves to sleep when the water was calm,
slowly rising when love seeped through the crevices of her skin,
stitching themselves into the dark raw purple of her scars,
holding her through every heartbeat

that she could've collapsed within,
gently egding themselves into the entirety of her
being until they became one.

She knew she was alive when she began
feeling her pulse vibrating through the anatomy of
her body,

becoming her own harmonious symphony,

creating melodies with the tapping of her
feet and dancing of fingertips,
the music entering her body found a home within,
becoming one, she slips into a trance of peace.

This dance with life is intended to be joyous,
we must learn to dance with all of our seasons,
inviting in every drop of rain and every ray of
golden sun.

*Feeling intensly has never been a curse
but it is a gift.*

As She Falls, She Rises

She dances amongst wild flowers,
feeling petals evaporating as they land upon her flesh,
she begins to see the whirlwind of beauty that
she has created herself to be,

oh the masterpiece of art is she,

decorating her being in poetry,
unfolding her wings as she guides
herself back to the roots of who she has always been,

wild

and

free.

Travelling back to the sweet humming of love
today is painted in gray, it's quiet on this train
but my mind is loud and my body is awake

here I am

here I stay

perfectly placed within this space

tuned in to the wholeness of me
tapped in to the power of being so free

oh what bliss it is to see with clarity.

As She Falls, She Rises

Her pulse begins to beat a little quicker as it keeps
up with the timing of the music,
words begin to crumble as she choreographs dance
routines in her mind,

smelling sweet perfume from strangers placed around her,

racing past green and brown hues,
the fields swallow her whole,
her eyes crack open to find she's walking through a
fairytale of trees,

content
she nestles in.

As She Falls, She Rises

Grey skies would usually pull me down, but today they lift me up
I remember the gift it is to witness all of this.

Happiness becomes unsustainable without life form surrounding you

every rain drop, every sun beam, every storm, every heart beat,
life creates life you see, it is all a joyous miracle dancing right in front of our faces,

yet we've become too consumed by our minds our lives,
flying to and from different places, open spaces
to really look at the miracle of this growing life
imagine yourself to be flying through space, you'll think you've won the race

before realising there was nothing to chase, but only time,
now a vast contrast of everything yet nothing, no real life form to see,

a beautiful contradictory,
one with the cosmos,

but no where to breathe, only here will you see that Earth will always be

home.

We must exist with life to remember the importance of our own.

When you're cloaked in darkness
learn to not be afraid of what the light looks like,
some say to never look directly at the sun,

but in a metaphoric way,

look as deeply and fearlessly as you can.

Feeling yourself wither and wilt until your petals dry up
crumbling into the depths of darkness wallowing below
                              disintegrating into dust

means you will one day witness your roots climbing
beyond heights you thought you'd never succeed in reaching.

You are growing and evolving in such a beautifully
profound way
becoming colours softer than a bed of feathers
your roots are melting into a river of soil
leaving a trail of kindness behind every step that you take.

We are here together, helping, guiding, assisting, shifting.

As She Falls, She Rises

Feeling myself falling
into a moment of delicious contentment
vibrating through music
there's a rhythm in my heart I attempt to find words amongst this peace
I hear no birds
or feel no wind dancing through the tangles of my hair

but I feel the call and pull from mother natures heart
pulling me back into the depths of her art
I dream of myself floating blissfully
amongst the glory of her waters.

As She Falls, She Rises

Rippling thoughts tangle in her mind
it seems she gets so tangled in the seaweed
that she
forgets to look up into the clear blue hues that cover the sky

the sand beneath climbs up her limbs
she dives deeper in
similar to how ivy wraps itself around anything that breathes
attempting to cling on so dearly
so it too can live free.
The current she is carried within reminds
her she's grounded even when she's afloat.

-Stay in flow, remind yourself it's okay to rewind and slow down,
soak in the glory of life,
feel it all,
see it all,
experience it all,
from one present moment to the next,
don't hold yourself back from the fullness of you.

Poem for Micheal

Lavender words, sweet succulent honey,
out of place in the space I stay, mundane days,
endless cups of coffee,
no seen gaps to spill the truth that drums
within me, until perhaps a soft conversation with a
familiar soul but a strangers face greets me,
painting the grey in lilac rays,
humble words held in truth, I cherish the
memories of unspoken warmth as I slip into
the tender presence of this days unfolding,
it is not often that I come across souls so
willing to speak from their heart,
so I intend for this poem to reach you with
words that are felt and perhaps not written,

the gentle gesture of kindness that you hold
is soft and something quite significant, thank you,
for your kind eyes and listening heart,
may all your days be coated in peace,
may you find joy in the subtle breeze that
reminds us all of the miracle it is to be able
to breathe.

You are exactly where you are supposed to be
every moment sacred
every moment soft
each moment a beautiful lesson for you to grow
from.

When things appear dark, breathe through the pain
allow yourself to feel, to crumble
allow yourself to *be* in the dark

but don't let it swallow you
don't let it drown you

instead let it rebuild you
as you reclaim
the fullness of you
the fully expressed

unapologetically undressed
you.

Any darkness you may be experiencing or have experienced, is not, never has been and never will be your identity.

Your light remains bold within, even when you can't feel or see it, know that there are others who can, you always come back to the truth of you.

You deserve to wake up happy.

-Think about it, really and truly dive into your existence, what
do you believe in?
Look up to the stars, look inside nature,
the divine source of all surrounds us,
you are held within the frequency of love.
Look to mother nature for guidance.

As She Falls, She Rises

There's a mellow hum of havoc travelling through my
my mind,
I piece together strands of pain, aching for the words
I receive to unravel the riddle within me,
I recklessly move myself into dancing poetry,
captivated by my own philosophy,
I ponder on the existence of life and how we've found ourselves
so bound by the disastrous rules of how to move so carefully,
the constrictions have always confused me,
eyes too wide to not see clearly,
do not lie to me,
I whisper to the tailing grip of my minds speech,
conditioned by this ridiculed society,
three dimensional reality,

do you not see the fear it pleads to feed humanity?

Inhaling the beauty that surrounds us all daily,

dreaming of the silent drum that echoes fluently through the horses of the sea,

the ocean bellows for me to surrender into the free flowing river in which we breathe.

As She Falls, She Rises

Turning words into jungles
walking through fields of magic

holding onto my heart as I feel my pulse beat

trusting soft water is coming

breaking through concrete soil

expanding these roots

releasing brittle petals

drifting into a collective awakening,

rising as one,
our voices are heard,

our souls are received

returning to unity

remembering to just be

Stuck in dreams of paralysis,
calling out for my body to come back,
inhaling dreams I know aren't real,
stoned in fear as my body lies limp and unresponsive,
waking up in a terror of panic,
fearing I've been taken back a few years,
silently screaming smothered in sheets,

trauma still attempts to invade my memory.

- Instead of an invasion of memories I let myself remember whilst holding my own hand through the feelings and sensations appearing, for I know the release and teaching are one in the same.

Nestled peacefully within the cracks of my heart,
falling comfortably into the rivers of my mind,
flowing fruitfully with no set direction,
waiting for the tide to pull me in as I let go of
resistance and slip into trust,
gravity forces everything that is golden warmth into me.

-Words flood through, I can't keep up with the pace in
which words spill through my mind, I bring myself to an
abrupt halt, stopping to re-focus back *in* on my breath, words
continue to fall, but at a slower pace as if letters are rain drops
creating streams, my words return to water as they
cascade through me, *descending perfectly into place*, feeling
stories behind each word. I cherish the unravelling, plunging
deeper into each word as I type or write.

Practice a meditation of some sort today, quieten your mind.
Meditation doesn't have to be you sitting crossed legged
repeating omms all over the place, it can be sitting in quiet
focusing on the sound of your breath, listening to high
frequency music, letting your creative self go wild, being
deeply present in nature, massaging your body, repeating
positive affirmations for yourself, meditation can be anything
that soothes the chit-chatter in your head and brings you back
to the present moment instead. You will thank yourself one day.

As She Falls, She Rises

Eyes flicker in between the dusted light,
scared to look too deeply in case we realise we are all souls being carried by bodies,

if we all took the time to study one another's eyes I wonder how many
starved souls would come home to love and light,

what is it we're all so afraid of,
seeing one another for who we are?

But isn't that the gift, isn't that the joy, seeing one another through the lens of truth,
isn't that really what we should teach and preach,

no more games that keep us playing in fear,

stuck in a state of amnesia turning utopia into inferno.

Life is bliss, do you not remember this?

- Breathe in through your nose for 6 seconds, hold it for 1 second then release for 6 seconds, repeat this a handful of times to calm your mind.

Feel your truth

    speak your truth

        regardless of who is listening

Unlock the cage that suffocates you
for you are golden light that deserves to flood entire galaxies

you are here creating how you see and experience your reality in every now moment

guiding yourself back to the home within,
we walk ourselves into our own awakening,

the rhythm of your pulse is where your spirit resides

follow the drum.

We go through our lives searching for ourselves in strangers
then we slowly learn to realise that through
pain and suffering
happiness and joy
we find ourselves,

in the twisting process we start to understand we are who we have always been searching for.

Spend more time alone,
be inquisitive about the person you have shaped yourself to be
eye gaze with those portals of yours.

Nature is narcotic for healing,
you'll learn more about yourself in the leaves that hide amongst trees then you will looking inside another person.

Paint yourself in colour

pour your heart into everything you do

whether you are laughing or crying,

feel into it all.

-You know how when you are laughing so much it hurts,
or when music makes you feel so good that you just have
to dance, well when you are experiencing anger, sadness,
anxiety, depression etc, allow your body to feel it the
same way you do when you are laughing, make peace with
what is passing, try not to hold on to it, rather witness
yourself feeling it through your body as you let go into flow.

Slipping into nimbus clouds
water droplets bend their way around my body
floating amongst mist
I feel myself held inside a humble clasp
in the palms of water,

I am cleansed with peace
in my dreams I find purified release
carried through pines
turning me into rain
we begin our journey to nourish and replenish earth

landing on the ground as *one*.

As She Falls, She Rises

Surrendering myself to the sand filled with footprints
placed in front of me, colourless clouds shadow me,
a soft rain reminds me it's okay to feel as I adsorb each
cleansing droplet,
the sea roars in the distance but I feel *her* close to my skin,
I stand in awe of the beauty that this moment holds,
with a delicate mind and an acheing heart
I softly notice that I'm stood exactly where I am supposed to be
the journey of becoming more me.

Stood cold on a wall, held in stillness whilst tears glisten in the
depths of my ocean green eyes.

Growth can hurt,

but then it pours liquid gold in the form of warm
rain that welcomes you to your skin,
no more harsh weather to feel lost within,
sunshine soars through
you
overflowing with contentment,
spilling love from your soul to all the souls you meet.

We experience growing pains so that we can feel
our strength.

You are growing more than just flowers

you are growing your own garden of Eden.

You   are   rare

As She Falls, She Rises

Birds fly as I pass by rolling hills
the silhouette of their wings
touches the clouds and evaporates into the thin
orange hues paint the sky
free to roam
I peer into the stream of this sunsetting fire
leaking through the gaps up high
I peer through the window to my left as life unfolds in clear
sight
words reveal themselves
elegantly
a tunnel pulls me inward to a silence that greets me
welcoming me to my own epiphany
here I land in my feet.

Peel back the layers of your self limitating mind,

empty your fear into the divine swirl of your creative eyes.

You are whole within.

Life is a pouring river of unconditional love,
as the water falls across rocks and pulls trees from
their once solidified roots,
they are carried weightless against everything,
held by the divine flow of something beautifully
uncontrolled.

You are water, flow with it.

You are a mirror of your own light,
no one else has the ability to save you,
only the ability to help guide you back to you,

become the blue skies that blindly guide you through

the grey in your mind.

You are growing through this process,
so yes there's a little rain, but this is essential for your growth,
water is the foundation of life.

Perhaps you're in a storm and everything feels uneasy,

lean into trusting it will pass and believe that a
beautiful sky is opening for you.

As She Falls, She Rises

Smoke dissipates into the air
disappearing out of sight,
the alchemy begins its first dance in the night
grounding into earth with every present step that presses
connected to thy chi an invisible stream of energy
A becoming, a reclamation, a bold movement into the truth
of what ripples through and emanates out
I play with the sea and embrace how she captivates the shadow of me that has
incarnated into a being of light
fully exposed
I created a sacred home
an open skylight to remind me these bones are a divine masterpiece
modeled by stardust

My body has remembered to move in a state of surrendered prayer
deeply present for the unravelling of my souls full expression
Liberty is what I call her
a rose always in bloom
a reborn meteor wearing a human suit
I am here, racing past, eating the fruits
blue skies drip ecstasy
clouds captivate the honey suckle in my sweet tea
rolling hills ripple euphoric energy into thy being
a reclamation so strong the amnesia of humanity better prepare for a love fueled war
to peel hearts wide open and pour truth through
we are here
angels have landed
light beings know who they are.

Dear this fear entangled society you better buckle in as you begin your ride to the
embers of earths fire
no more of your ridiculed propaganda
you thought you stood a chance against the infinite love that we know we are?
Did you want to make us laugh because millions of us are
humoured by the pathetic grip that you so attempt to hold
the tables haves turned
the power is within us
now fully embedded into our own flower bed

minds speech is losing the literacy it preaches
ready to roar with the lioness of the storms
the cosmic blanket of infinity
we have *remembered* ourselves
choosing to be all in
fully *live*

you can't see our wings? Well trust that they are there.

It's you and it's me
returning to our ancestors teachings
our being is water
more powerful than the mind can comprehend

a new energetic realm has landed upon Earth
we are spinning through portals, can't you see?

Always been heaven
just separated by fear
but, *love is the medicine that we've all been taking*

integrating our past pains into lessons
no fakers
just peace makers
this is a happening

are you counting yourself in on this?

can *you* feel this?

Nestled within the cracks of my body,

following my soul as she sings to be heard,

dancing with life,
giving up the fight,

sleeping softly through the night,

everything is going to be alright.

We are all art,
choose how you create yourself.

Return to your heart

        return to your soul

                return home

Through pain you grow, emotions are our path to healing.

Allow emotions to flow freely
especially when they feel unwelcome and uneasy
learn to trust the process of your mind
hold the pain in a different light.

All is well
take your time
there is no race
it's all divine

It's time to stop depriving yourself of love
unleash the grip
let your heart open wide
empty the contents of what's inside

there's no room left to hide

this world needs you

exactly as you are
wherever you are

you are the light.

Movement is medicine,

allow your body to move in the way your
soul intends for you to
in perfect rhythm
with the pulse that
drums
through
constantly guiding you.

-Through surrendering and allowing my body
to move in any way, shape or form, I
met myself in a different light, I leaped
directly into my own silhouette, twirling
into the shadowed parts of me that always
intended to be set free.

A sea breeze kisses my skin as the sun begins to rise into the day
I give my gratitude for the way my life is shaped
I am a soft feathered owl who isn't afraid of transforming into an eagle
I fly
I soar.

The way butterflies orchestrate the way they dance upon the
surface of the oceans skin is beyond me
they remind me of the way I move so freely
wildly calm in the presence of *simply just* being
here to be the buttercup
a flower that's always in bloom
untethered
unshaped
a ghost in a room

my heart beat emanates love with ease

join me in being who you came here to be.

As She Falls, She Rises

Your mind is a meadow full of wild flowers and humming birds,

rivers and mountains,

streams and creaks,

care for the earth that your bare feet walk upon,

dance in the long grass and sing with the angels that soar through the azure delights.

You are free to be free.

                                        You are free to be free
You are free to be free.

                    You are free to be free.

                                        You are free to be free

You are free to be free.

                                        You are free to be free

You are free to be free.

There are some days when we must allow for the rain to soak in

encouraging each falling droplet to cleanse what is stagnant within

releasing what no longer belongs just as a snake sheds its skin

growing into your wings

following the rhythm

surrendering to the ocean as you remember how to swim.

Abundance feeds me vegan brownies
with a hint of the remains of French pastry
sipping on a coffee that my lover has
made for me
life is complete

I find myself happy here
open here

walking home beat after beat
I change the tempo of my feet
matching the rhythmic flow of lifes
sweet treats

ebbs and flows
I am dancing home.

As She Falls, She Rises

You are more than the skin and bones that hold you,
you are more than the name that labels you,
you are more than the identity you've shaped yourself into.
Life is a gift don't you see?
It is a miraculous blessing that you are even here,
think about the perfection of your human design,
held to the ground by gravity as your soul soars beyond the sky,

you are light   you are life   you are alive

that's enough you see

 all you need to do is be.

As She Falls, She Rises

We all have someone who inspires us to keep on going
despite the treacherous uneven shapes beneath our cut off tongues and weary faces
we see this light in others eyes
pulled into their divine spark
not noticing the gaps inbetween where we're really meeting our own gaze gleaming
just reflecting in another's skin, porcelain, melanin

listening for the drum that we believe is outside until the night closes in and we're left
without   a   shooting   star   to   wish   our   pain   away   on
the troubles that we grappled with were never truly ours to carry alone in the dark.

Letters dance amongst cobbles
we're reading riddles
feeling into the holy bible of our minds
we are our own guiding disciples
three wise men, oh the chuckle
the scripture is an interpretation of the stars held within Akasha
ethereal elements keep us turning

so what if that someone that we aspire to breathe like is really our own guides
our own light
that has forever remained inside the beating lamp that connects us to the heavens that
we've fallen to believe we are separate from

palm in palm here
your neighbor is dear so love others and keep them near

see the divine not the divide.

Unveil the restraints that hold you

you came here to see the truth and be the
truth

you came here to create all that you dream

you came here to breathe into the whole of your being.

As She Falls, She Rises

Skip hold
breathe slow
pulse pulse

set the tempo
blue blankets the sky willingly
telling a story of liberty
reminding us we are free to be exactly who we intended to be
no limits
no tide too wild to diminish me
the sea mimics the strength in thee
blue hues are made up of waves
see the connection
the sea is blue because of reflection

birds chirp to the willow tree
she tells me to create my own melody of
gardens that are wildly pristine

ahead of the game what a heavenly way to
weather their reign

untethered you claim joy as your birthright

no more battles for a loveless war
we return to new waters.

So elegantly content,
a golden warmth pours through this body I'm learning to create a home for,
gracefully spinning through portals of love,
I find myself dancing with darkness, but choreographing light.

-Moving in no specific way, rather just surrendering and letting my soul move my body has been incredibly healing for me, I encourage you to move in any way today, it does not matter what you think you might look like or if you think you can't dance. I dance when I don't know how else to move with the emotions I'm experiencing, when it's so intense inside that I feel like I'd rather die than see the emotions through, I move, no control, no rules.

Let your spirit move you.

Movement is medicine.

Lilac silk covers my skin,
my wings tangle with growing flowers,
the ghost of my being disintegrates into dust,
as the moon shines it shatters every ounce of past pain
that still remain in the depths of my mind,
preparing to propel me forward,
disseminating the soot into the sunset,
taking my soul to a beautiful sunrise,

starting anew within this body I'm remembering to call my home.

Stay in tune with the rhythm in your chest
surrender to it all as you fly from your nest
open your wings as you cascade through life in slow motion
feeling everything unfolding in divine timing
you are right where you are supposed to be
living from this now moment to the next.

Soak it all in
bath in the glory that is your life
honor your humanness and celebrate the very gift of being alive.

You are much more than what your trained mind wants you to see.

Dance in the mundane grey and sing in the hues of blue.

Strip away your given identity, who do see yourself to be really?

As She Falls, She Rises

She shrivelled herself into depression
and suffocated herself in ivy
bending her bones over her skeleton body

to try and curve herself into some sort of forcefield

only to realise that she needed to leave her body in
order to come back home to herself.

Practice being with stillness,
look to nature for guidance,

listen to the soft humming of birds to find your own inner peace.

We are gently guiding one another home through rippling currents of love.

In each breath you are present for, you are shifting the collective energetics,

your breath and presence is more powerful than you can imagine.

Let natures whispering presence clear the film that covers your eyes,

see through the fog in your mind.

We can't force or hide emotions
they flow through us like a stream
sometimes a gushing stream that perhaps feels more like a tsunami
either way it flows through
stillness is coming and you are growing
you are here for it
showing up and doing it
despite the fog that comes and goes
the rain that turns into hail stones
you keep on walking because you believe in rainbows.

Know that you are never alone

your soul is always with you
for it is you

gently guiding you as you walk your walk with life.

This time is precious,
we are witnessing a universal rebirth.

Dripping into orchards
hoping my mind will get caught in the petals
taking new flowers with me into my growth.

Let it out
the emotions that have been climbing up your throat
aching to just turn into a stream and return to flow.

My mind is a garden,

I had planted seeds but the only growth I witnessed were growing weeds,
I sat looking ahead searching for petals
forgetting to look inside my head,

my mind is a garden, not the pristine type
wild flowers are over growing spilling into streams
lily pads float amongst pebbles and rocks
the water is clear yet somewhat soft,

my mind is a garden, but there is no gardener
grass grows untamed
collecting climbing bugs and bees
weeds are not pulled from the ground
instead they grow their own wishing well
crafted from the dandelions spell

my mind is a garden
there is no limitation to my growth
trees grow amongst mountains
rivers overflow
the whispering sea has become my haven
my mind is a garden in which I have found solace within.

As I dip and pour gracefully into the depths of the unknown
abyss below
I find my reflection rippling beneath
she asks me to *slow down*
to feel my heart beating
to notice my breathing,

I hadn't realised that as I told others to breathe I had
forgotten how to myself.

-There are still times that I find myself drowning in my own tears, my own sadness, my own desperation for joy and no more nothingness/numbness, there are still moments when I ache in depressions grip and fall loosely... or rather heavily to the floor....to my knees, until I weep all that is left of me, cheeks burnt from the salt water rivers that cascade from me, there are still times when I feel intensely, but the difference is I am not dismantling myself in the process, not hating myself, shaming myself, rather I'm learning to love all parts of me,

I am her listener
her mother
her friend
her guide
I am all that she is
yet I remain quiet as I observe the mind.

It is our personal duty to balence the mind, body and soul as one, in doing this we are serving ourselves, yet in serving ourselves with love and intention we offer the collective a reminder of the importance of this work, the more we choose love, the more love humanity will receive, the more love humanity receives the more we will all begin to see, the more humanity sees, the more we will remember unity.

Life is magic
open your mind and see through what you can see
breathe yourself into the moment
that's where you will find peace
nothing external will bring you what you seek
only you can give yourself what you need

s l o w   d o w n

breathe   in   breathe   out

The ocean is where I find solace

water is the foundation of all life.

I wish I could give you
a glimpse
of how
incredible you are
trust these words
when I say

one day you will see,

one day you will know
your own beauty
I don't mean what you look like
although you look wonderful

I mean your heart
I mean what's inside
the life behind your eyes

you will see it all

I promise that
in choosing
to love
and to honour
yourself
it will
transform
your own inner world
and you
will remember
why
you breathed yourself to life
in the first place.

Take the first step today
whisper
i love you
to yourself
or heck shout it out
recognise the skin that *holds you*
see the body
that *you* exist within

look into your own eyes

give yourself a hug

hold your own hand

there is no better love than the love we can give ourselves.

As She Falls, She Rises

I find myself floating beneath the oceans skin
feeling my entire life dripping off of me
my cheeks slowly pierce through the water
surrounding my limbs

my eyes begin to open

rippling blues roll ahead
mountains plant themselves in the distance
threads of clouds are painted above

it clicks
and
I remember the mermaid within.

Holding gratitude for whom I witness myself to be
feeling nostalgia as memories slip beneath

I grip on to every lasting moment
knowing that what is
is all that will ever be

no past
no future

just this momentary bliss.

I stride inward
quieting the stream of thoughts
that trickle,
honing in closer
to holding love
for all
that is,

this *angelic soul* guides me
softly
reminding me
to clasp my mind with gentle pulsations of
intimate acceptance.

I welcome in the storms
the emotions that ripple,
releasing attachment
but
remaining still
as I observe each compelling heart
beat,

cradling the shadow as I dance along side her
working for peace as I walk with others on Eden

breathing *in*
freedom.

As She Falls, She Rises

Water surrounds her holding no temperature
as though silk is dancing upon her skin
undergoing some sort of angelic bath
the ocean barely ripples as she rises to the surface
she pulls her ribs in trying to create a pool for the water to bathe in
breathing in softly
making sure to fill her entire body
exhaling deeply as she releases everything that no longer nourishes her.

-Through these breaths I begin to *feel inside* my body again,
I remember I have toes that can wiggle and a voice that deserves to be heard.

My mind is soft and calm
each day
tender and sweet
freedom is the language in which I speak

I clasp on to each moment checking in with my own rhythm
feeling into where my mind is
ensuring she is present with the presence of all that is.

Spirit is omnipresent.

The presence of perfection always exists
it is the mind that is tampered with.

Trust your innate wisdom
ignite your roaring soul and hear
all that is being delivered to you

live from moment to moment

hone into the truth of you.

You and I are the receiver of
thoughts and feelings from the
creator within

release attachment to your ego lens
instead observe and learn
as you invite in
your full expression

feel into the pulse that drums
through

breathe into the breath that breathes you.

Each day captures a different story of rebirth and remembrance
messages filled with potency spill *and* crumble
into poetry
I listen closely
to the language of nature
my mind falls quiet
I enable my hearts voice to drip into my awareness with grace
learning to communicate with my inner self
words never spoken yet profoundly felt.

I let go into this unravelling life

seeing clearly
feeling intensely
living unapologetically
loving unconditionally.

- I reclaim myself *here*
I commit to myself *here*
I know my strength has kept me breathing *here*.
In my darkest hardest moments I learnt
that I had to accept that I was strong enough to carry on in order for
the emotions to pass.

You are strong enough to get through whatever you are growing through right now.

Remember to *breathe* into the depths of *you*

hold yourself with love through everything that appears
surrender to the thrilling mystery that is your life

you are held on earth
made from perfection
breathe in
exhale out

as you take another breath in
listen closely
to the voice within,
trust the trickling
words
of love
that sing

Can *you* remember who *you* are?

Unravel into the soft water that surrounds you
float in the calm of this breeze
all is well in the presence of remaining present

release attachment
the crashing of these waves will bring you succulence and life

may you arise fluently in tune with the rising sun
and rest peacefully when the day is done

you are one
as am I
as are we

collectively we breathe.

The new 'normal' is a conscious society
accepting of all
for we remember
we are one.

See the blossoming crinkles surrounding your eyes as a reminder of all of the times you have smiled.

Fairy dust blankets the night sky,
we make our wishes and send them off into the moonlight.

We ache for the life we are already living
distracted by the mundane life that we've been constructed to live within

unveil the restraints that are failing to contain you
you were never meant to fit yourself into one shape

you are fire and water
the sun and the moon

you are more than the skin that is your home
you are more than what you can see

feel the resonance of truth

everything is always working out for you
every experience is a lesson to guide you towards expanding your consciousness
your growth is inevitable and *you* are forever eternal.

Nothing is everything and everything is nothing,
life is a movie and you are the creator, the narrator, the director,
life is a movie and you are the observer dropping in,
embodying this whole human...thing.

Poetry has been lingering in a quiet place these past few days,
my writing has changed as have I,
I open my wings,
soaring with confidence as I fly even higher into the depths of this sky,
I want to be soft, but I want to be heard,
I want to be loud, but I want to be gentle.

I can not unwind this linear time and re-deliver what has already arrived,
every letter that falls holds its own story,
I re-write these words to accentuate their meaning,

I want to be soft, but I want to be heard,
I want to be loud, but I want to be gentle,

so I will be both
the river and the storm,
colliding into one as the ocean continues to roar,
held within my essence
I feel I should write something more poetic,
but then I question what is poetry anyway,
I conclude that it is an orchestrated painting of words with an open
invitation for another soul to peak into,
to dive into,
to feel whatever arrives because they are free to do so,
poetry is a painting and each colour is received uniquely.

I love the unknown of this medicinal mystery.

As She Falls, She Rises

Soaking in water I sit patiently
awaiting for the divine to move me
silk is my skin
here is the brim of what I leave open and no longer closed

Soul fully expressed   fully exposed

is the lesson I've been grappling with
but I no longer entertain the plotted mind game
become my slave I say as I move forward in grace
maybe I am anomaly but only to the eyes that do not *see* me
fog in the night carried into the day
clarity cleanses the thought through pain that can only be felt outside of a present state
when you awake from your life lived dream you will be proudly gleaming in the joy of earths rhythm
here to say you made it through the days that you once thought were impossible
hand on your heart you remember the true art of being *live* for the life surrounding

we sit in pause in an energetic replay
the constellations are our news feed
look up
not down
the paper is a distraction from the truth of what's really happening

it's Jupiter and Saturn
not Boris or Biden
that's brave I say as I humor at the facade that we're all been playing characters in

don't you know Esme is not my name
I am a being of light
breathing a human
making a home in her skin

Zodiacs inform us of whom is compatible
not invincible
don't swallow those capsules they are bate for an uncharitable experiment
money making government

I spill truth what will they do?

As She Falls, She Rises

The algorithm is questionable
poisonous fear injects through new policy's
but don't they know we already knew the truth

fooling us with their hypocrisy

look to your oracles to deliver to you the silver foods of what your soul consumes

love does not create any trouble
paddle paddle
light is digestible
open your crown and you will feel the consciousness rushing through your root

let yourself breathe to ignite your bodys anatomy

close your eyes
step out of time
connect with your guides
your galactic race
the pleiadians say *i love you*
keep walking
keep your heart open
for that will clear the contents of the man-made maze out of your vision

follow your intuition

how close can you listen?

Don't attach, just feel

feel the emotion flowing through
dance away the stagnant energy that may remain in your body

you are here to experience it all

allow for life to unfold in tune with you

remember that you too are as fundamental as the orbiting moon.

As She Falls, She Rises

Gently rising into another life
the light of today is seeping through the blinds

unravelling itself into this tapestry haven
hearts beating slow as the dreams of last night trickle
away
music flows through my body
dancing to the shape of the colours
that are waiting to be painted.

Choose the colours you paint your days with,
but never carry the same canvas as yesterday

all there is
is today.

Water your seeds with awareness of what you are growing.

-When we search our minds to try and find the reason behind why an emotion may have begun to rise, we often create attachments to whatever it may be, meaning the emotion may linger for longer and you are more likely to manifest more of that emotion into your reality, as it is all vibrational,
the universe doesn't hear your words, it feels the energy behind them and whatever you are feeling the universe responds with more of that,
so whatever you give your attention to is what you are watering the seeds of.

Re-focus where your thoughts are and check in to make sure they are in alignment with your highest self, don't judge where your mind is at, simply observe as you bring your attention back to the things that make you feel content with ease.

When you feel emotions rising, embrace, observe and accept them for what they are, hold peace for yourself as the emotion passes, rather than attaching to it and trying to 'fix' it.

As She Falls, She Rises

The morning mist blankets over the rolling hills
grey clouds rise high
nature is a constant reminder to stay present for all that is
honouring and observing the light *and* the dark
but finding solidity within remaining soft in the harsh weather
the sky may be grey today
in tune with my mind or perhaps
it is
the other way around.

I surrender to my soul as I land back to the ground
I remember all is well as I stand with my feet pressed firmly beneath
breathing back into my center as I *feel* the pulse in my neck

We belong here
living from one moment to the next

As She Falls, She Rises

She peers through her ocean green eyes
witnessing her life
she orchestrates a dance as she moves with her body
words flow
she doesn't fiddle trying to find the meaning.

Her soul whispers *presence*
she unveils the shadowed parts of her
softly shedding her skin and replacing her bare body
with feathers

She sleeps in silk
waking in tune with the sun rise
light ripples through her blinds
the sky *is* beautiful
glowing angelic light

the ocean roars
inviting her in
she grabs her board and follows the calling.

-Writing out my dreams as I patiently wait for them to unravel into my reality. You have the power to manifest all that you dream, there is nothing that is out of your reach.

It is safe to heal

it is safe to start loving yourself the way you deserve to be loved.

Time has been moving quickly it seems
trickling beneath
as if a stream
words within me
I await for you now
to make sense of these empty fingertips
with no tales to tell

1111 I land back in
to the vessel that *is me*
esme

-Angels are speaking, are you listening?

I drift into nirvana as paint spills from this vessel
I pour myself into the art that I create
no guidelines or rules
just easy flowing strokes
each lick of paint tells its own story

absorbed in the colour that is spilling from my mind

I am alive.

Look through what you can see.

As She Falls, She Rises

Time is not something recorded by a clock
the tick-tock is something humans invented
perhaps to separate us
from what is truly god

I use the term god to describe something
that can not be named
the universal energy that creates all and is all

presence is all we breathe in

the mind holds memory of the past and future
in attempt to distract us
from the perfection
of what is
right here and now

Slip into this moment
feeling your fingertips
brush across the page you read
feel your feet wherever they may be planted

watch your breath breathe.

As She Falls, She Rises

Here I sit
accompanied by the pitter-patter
of these falling letters
the sound that the keyboard makes drums into my ears
the chirping sound of crickets hum in the background

I reflect on my time spent occupied with the present moment
engaging in conversations with people who have
never truly been strangers

nature is soft as it is wild
gentle as it is fierce

my mind awaits for poetry to seep through
as my body whispers for me to sleep

I am in awe of the cluster of what I see life to be

I share secrets with the moon as my eyes close
drifting into
another dream.

Attend to the flowers planted in your mind
treat your garden with grace
love the weeds you pull from the soil

love the thorns
the thistles
the snails
the butterflies
love it all
remember the test of choosing to love even when it rains

do not stop to listen to the thunder, but dance with it

join in with the storm
roar with appreciation for feeling so deeply
for experiencing life so intensely.

Love yourself like never before.

Life is a test of love

we are the pupils of remembering how to choose love even when we are faced with pain and fear.

Life is a classroom that we constantly attend taking notes as we learn and grow.

As She Falls, She Rises

We carry a backpack of identities
slipping into a certain character
depending on the energetic environment we are in
whether this be a place or a person

but what if we took this backpack of personalities off of our shoulders
and walked freely for a little while
what if we stood bare and naked as who we came here to be
no more layers to break through just to find the truth

what if we didn't coat ourselves in stories
but instead we *could* just be
with presence
and allow for the words that trickle into our minds to be spoken and felt
instead of misheard and judged

what if we ask without expecting to hear an answer

but instead we felt it
through listening and feeling into our bodies language?

-After years and years of being redirected from our truth, the walk
back home may feel treacherous to begin with, but we will always
come back to the remembrance of who we are.

I've been wading through fog
barely remembering how to breathe
I wonder how it is possible for a day to feel so impossible to get through
sometimes it gets really dark inside my mind
even when the sun is shining clear and bright
I peer into the clouds aching to feel even a little alive
but all I find are aching cries

I cried so much I created a pool for myself to drown in

until I remembered I *could* swim
I *could* rise
I *could* fly

if i wanted to....

It is all a choice you see
for me this has been the scariest part of stepping forward
into
who I really be
we are the controller of our lives

yet we were taught to look outside

which leaves us screaming in daylight
begging for the night to arrive
to swallow the tides of our mind.

As She Falls, She Rises

I intend to be a voice for those who feel unable to speak
for I have also been a silent teacher
battling a war within my own mind against myself with no where to hide and only pain to confine in
I stripped myself bare of food of water of love of laughter
I crippled in despair as I awaited for my own abomination to take place
I waded through aching days that I tried so desperately to climb out of
choking in my own suffocation as I ripped my skin to shreds
death became an embodiment and I walked myself there
no rights just rules and restraints
bright blue lights and no way of escaping I've been there
drowning in my own abyss
reaching a bottomless pit
I fought for death as my body fought for its life
I know the pain all to well to ever go back there.
So here I strengthen my grip to my pen as I prepare to give my truth a voice
for others to find a way out of their despair
you will survive this
the rain may feel like blades of ice
ripping through everything that could have been nice
I understand the irradical weather
but here I speak so one day you may too,
soften your heart into your creative art
as you allow for the real you to come through
let these words be a portal of love that hold you in your truth
I intend to remind you that you are not loco or too far gone
don't let the system fool you
your wisdom is saving you
focus on that voice that murmurs
let that be the guidance that pulls you *inward*
the medicine is there, but
it is not in the thrill of living between a state of manic appeal to that suicidal ideal
it is here in the presence of your open heart
not your closed mind
open your third eye
let the truth inside
you will get through this
you are going to be alright

we learn things in the dark that the light will not teach us.

Be the example of love that you came here to be.

Choose love

Oh the hustle and bustle
of balancing on the tight rope of this human life
one foot in front of the other
arms spread wide preparing for flight

it is when we wobble
it is when we curl into the darkness that we forget
we are the light

or not necessarily forget but lose touch of.

We are walking this tight rope of life
stumbling here and there
dancing amongst the light as we tiptoe through the dark
carefully placing our steps as we remember to love
the tender gift of
being so human

being so real

so free
so raw
so true

Remember to be you
you are like no other
you are rare
you are unique
you are worthy

You are *essential* for this dance with life.

As She Falls, She Rises

Capturing memories in our fingertips
as they slip slip slip and evaporate into mist
feel into where you are
be in the unknown

Gifted life
as if it were as simple as creating a light bulb
forgetting this was seen as impossible once upon a time

only a clock will tell what has been created with a human mind.

Moving with the wind
holding
gripping
releasing

surrendering
further in
to love

pulling what has not been seen
to the surface of my crystal clear eyes

unveiling what screams to be heard

I listen

in

As She Falls, She Rises

We chase feelings
not places nor people
we run from moments that call us to settle into
the slow unfolding motion

in fear of running out of time

we run through life like a leopard appaloosa
trying to put the puzzle together until we realise
the pieces have always fit.

You deserve to give yourself your own love

We spit and spew words
in fear of giving truth a voice

exchanging mindless babble to pass by time

keeping *masks up* hoping no one will see the souls within us

but we're all the same

running away
from the fear consciousness that we label as society
gasping for air
as we look back at how far we have travelled without even blinking an eye
because we forgot *we are a life*

so busy being fed lies
becoming more and more afraid of life

until one day it stops
we realise we can not run anymore
because there is no place to hide

this moment is when self realisation appears,

pay close attention to the orchestration of life.

She passes smiles to strangers daily
gifting everyone with a presence of angelic nature
lifting others that are starving for life to breathe through them again
falling into tranquility
she exhales a moaning sigh of relief.

Don't give up here

not now you've come this far

keep on breathing through the passing of these storms.

You've got to start seeing everything surrounding you
as an unfolding miracle
in order to remember
you
are the miracle
itself.

Let go
release

don't hold back
don't hold on

witness what is
find the beat of your pulse

-Take a couple of moments for yourself to breathe deep, feel the pulse within you.

Can you give yourself this moment to be still?

As She Falls, She Rises

Dearest brothers and sisters do not let the system dim us
shine clear into the day
don't hide your truth
don't shy away
the downloading of your consciousness is a gift to this humanity
see through the polarity, insanity

dearest brothers, dearest sisters
I see you
the algorithm can't contain you, nor shape you
you are the rainbow colours that we move through
I'm tired of these rhymes but this message wants to find you
to the one who is afraid of saying yes to life
of embracing your own tide and controlling the rambling of your mind
I am here with you.

Dearest sisters and brothers we are doing just fine
lighting up the entire world with our own light

forget believing and move into knowing

for you are the truth
the illusions are pixelating
people are realising the game we're playing
we can't run away from the united agenda
we are one, it is a matter of remembering this
the dark matter is

you and I a breathing aspect of the multiverse

every molecule, every particle, every atom is this
the divine source exists in and at our fingertips

dearest brothers and sisters you only momentarily forgot this
so open your heart as you come back to the infinite knowledge that is within all of us

we are the universe.

As She Falls, She Rises

Reflecting on love
pretending there is no time between his pulse and mine
we know we collide

unified
purified

these words bring attention to my mind
I keep my eyes wide

open I find

the clock has ticked and my heart beat twice.

Creating a waterfall of movements
feeling the trickle of magic cleansing my soul
climbing these branches ready to teach these wings how to fly

pearly white strokes placed upon lilac clouds

free to be human
free to be.

As She Falls, She Rises

We imprison ourselves to a form of human captivity
shaping our minds into chaos as we put the blame on society
but really it's just you and me
wading upstream
telling ourselves we will never be free
living in an overflowing river of uncertainty

until we surrender to the stream and open our eyes to see with clarity
no identities to label you nor me

remember you have always been free.

You don't get bored of something you love.

Carried weightless in waves

trust in the weather of you

know that your body always knows what to do

you can't control the weather you grow through
but you can choose how to dance in it.

There is so much beauty to be felt
to be seen
to be received
in where you are right now

look up
can you feel yourself rise?

Moving as if oneself is in orbit
undeniably committed
to circling around our own hearts.

-Have you ever stayed as an observer to your own breath?

Her hands start to shake
there's a rippling affect that he creates
she's glued to the way her heart dances
when his presence is scattered around the place.

The bravest thing you can do is carry on.

You cradled me with an empty love
your hands gently stroked through the tangles of my hair
your voice was a false medicine
I became addicted to your taste
I could've stayed there forever
still within a moment
that felt like a race.

-If you are reading this and you find yourself in a relationship that makes your heart sink a little further rather than gleam a little brighter, sit with yourself for a moment and just get clear on how you truly feel deep down in your beautiful heart, it's okay to choose yourself, please know that life will change and jump with you when you take those first steps and leaps in discovering, choosing and committing to you.

As She Falls, She Rises

You will see everything you want to see
you will experience the most incredibly profound moments
creating life saving memories
you will feel joy beating out of your heart
and in your entire vessel
you will see the most beautiful sunrises
sunsets
mountains
rivers
lakes and seas
sugar sun beam oh how you gleam
remember it's okay to melt
all a becoming of who you are truly here to be
each step an unravelling motion of gliding footprints
scattered across the earth for the rest of time
your energy remains deep in the cosmic sea

you are a thread of miracle energy
oh what a speck you are indeed

a glorious ball of fire dancing in the divine light
that breathes life into all that is seen and unseen
felt and untouched

you are energy pulsing a drum
playing a beat
you can not be defeated
life is designed for you to be in it
breathe in this truth
that has always been you.

Let go of fear
paint your path
in the colours your being is designed to breathe in

you are love

love is.

Driving through the rain
watering the day
cleansing my mind as I breathe into the soft music playing
window wipers paint a clean slate
my heart wonders un-chained
I clasp each word tenderly
my fingertips release their grip
one
by
one
glances of love as a new song changes the rhythm of our hearts collision
love is strong I whisper to myself discretely,
I breathe into my body
wiggling my toes to remember I belong

fog hits hard against the windscreen
lights glow dim as we speed past neighboring cars
new music drips into my mind
thumping
now I'm jumping
appearing new in naked skin
no more layers suffocating my crown
my root is strong as light cascades down.

Foreign music enters now
a language I don't know speaks to me
I ponder on how beautiful it is to be
living in a world where language causes us to speak without words
edging us to remember the subtle ways we communicate
we speak through our souls and interpret feelings for words
oh how beautifully extraordinary it is to live upon Earth.

Grow with grace.

Life is an open door waiting for you to step in and explore.

Clouds fall into the sky
pockets of lilac keep my gaze high
I feel into my essence
praying for guidance
I release my troubles
remembering I'm not alone in my struggles.

-The discomfort you may find yourself in is only momentary, yet it holds lessons that will last a lifetime, inner reflections of a mirrored external

life is a teaching of love.

The river flows with flowering abundance
the sheep lay low preparing for their morning melody of baa's
the birds are silent within their slumber
twigs and leaves pulled from their trees
the water continues to cascade

my eyes fall as I peer into this screen
holding on to these words
as I catch every falling shape
that constructs itself into a poetic painting

my eyes are tired as is my mind
humble love swoops in the dark midst of midnight

sleep tight
I whisper.

easing into the rise and fall
I remember the gift of moving through time.

As She Falls, She Rises

Eden isn't out of reach
Eden is here resting beneath the soles of our feet.

We walk around in unison
holding hands with strangers of whom become lovers
how funny it is
the movie we live within
we're taught to believe that this movie is something we are subject to playing in

climb out of your skin

dive *deeper*

soar high

dance with your soul to remember you are home.

As She Falls, She Rises

It can feel daunting at times
all this fear to dismantle
all this love to hand out
no touching of the fingertips allowed
without interaction we dissolve into our own oblivion
yet here we are
fighting a war without weapons
consciously walking with our wings up
held high
sprinkling snow upon the mountain tops
pine trees climb into the sky
dropping their cones to remind us of the sprial of life
Fibonacci
deluded by the hierarchy
fighting for unity
the patriarchy still believe in their authority
too many rhymes I gotta simplify
mellow hum of humans noise
get outside
listen to the sound of the sun crackling its fire
turning all of this into life
spinning through infinity at a speed we can't comprehend
never walking in the same space twice
what a precious gift to celebrate
inhale in jubilation
exhale
everything is all right
golden atmosphere
breath of the divine.

As She Falls, She Rises

My heart sinks deep

I notice myself noticing thee
I don't want to dance
I want to swim
with the currents of what's within
harboring in
the river in me
water falls still as I move
into
clarity

angelic guides whisper to me

you have always been free, it takes a choice to believe.

There is beauty in loving where you are right now.

Every time you speak your truth

it is the equivalent of angels singing

let your voice be heard and your soul be felt

your eyes contain rivers that make others melt

you are the soft lavender scents that send people into sweet dreams

you are the honey suckle dripping from a tree

be like the bear they say

soft and free, one with the wind

be childlike and play on swings

roar with the tide as the ocean peels your heart wide

open

follow the whispers of your soul

let yourself gleam

breathe into your body

reclaim the version of you

that you came here to unapologetically be.

Think about how long it takes for a willow tree to grow
apply that to your own growth
you too must take your precious time and gift it wisely
to the seeds you wish to sow.

Can you slow down into the presence of now and
water your mind with the love that you so deserve?

Heaven on Earth is a choice to see

we must redirect to where our hearts connect

to where our souls rest

re-focus your attention
to the bliss
of mother natures fountained existence

no stones throw needed
to come back to the glowing portal of love that we walk upon

open your heart and let your light beam upon humanity

a change in consciousness is fundamentally necessary

rest assured it is a continuous happening.

As She Falls, She Rises

Memories flood in
uncomfortably I remember the past versions of me
lovingly I accept who no longer wears a mask
perhaps not literally... we're playing in a facade
monopoly players of the elite attempt to contain us to this three dimensional society
a gimmick on humanity
or so it seems
society is the thief of the souls within you and me
skin to love not to play hide and seek with.
Different energetics blend into this tone
I feel a spring in my step yet I'm buried under my duvet at one with the bed
resting my head at 2:34 in the morning
but what is time I ponder again
but a manifestation of the fourth dimension
where memories can be fathomed
because we skip into the rhythm of our minds that remember other now moments
so it is a continuing of life unfolding
still the big bang happening
the divine breathing existence amongst all spaces
all faces
all molecules
all mountains
rivers and glaciers
all beings and animal races
all one in the same here.
A ploy to separate us from the only true way through this
essentially it's oneness
simply put *it is* love
sprinkled stardust dancing across the blanket above
angel dove it's *all* about love
this is the vibration we know how to speak
let us not be weakened by the unconscious living
instead offer a helping hand forgiving whatever monstrous treason attempted to teach
this sleeping being.
We must wake up with the children
supporting them as they strengthen the collective vision of earths harmonic rhythm.

Love her as she nurtures you
trust in the lessons of the unpredictable weather
must I remind you to dance in the rain?

As She Falls, She Rises

She is strong
she is free
her soul gleams
authentically fiery
bold to be breathing in naked skin
no layers to unveil
she left acting in duplicity
incarnated into liberty
a seasonal metamorphosis
is what she calls the phase of her Pisces moon.

She created a safe haven within the lungs of her being
integrating the vibration of her truest selfs essence
water is fluid
feather hands see to the meadows sowed upon land
eyes close softly as dreams fall gently into
her third eyes vision
reminiscing
the temple glistens in soft blue currents
her crown peels open
light waterfalls through the anatomy of her body
her breath leads her into her own presence

now flowing

she knows she is her own medicine.

Bow down to Mother Eden she will show you the way.

All a reflection of what you are
beautiful mystery your oceans are,
dazzling in lilac coral
your open heart is a portal.

As She Falls, She Rises

Take me to my oceans and free me of what's unwritten

transform my skin into silk as I bathe in mothers womb

deep in my bones
I remember I carry a beating sacred home

this is the vessel I breathe

transmit to me the secrets of the cosmos infinite sea

roar to me lioness of the storms

cradle me as I become reborn.

You have a way of *being*
yourself in such a wonderful way
so my dear
please listen to these words
when I say

you bring the wonder back
into strangers days
your gift is your gleam
that you so effortlessly give away

but remember
the sun
can't always stop the rain
so you too
must allow
your salt water rivers to cascade.

Your fresh start is here and now
follow the flow of the current
trust in the path that always leads you home

oh but home is a place that you never truly leave
a few breaths away from resonance in your chest
of who you have always been

no rein to be guided by the weight of the pull of
your arms

liberty is her name

potent images of a time spent with angelic guidance
gates into my mind
a beautiful friesian
wide eyed
blue eyes gazing into mine
water begins replenishing my wings

I swim through emerald lights
meeting the goddess slumbered peacefully
resting in a pearl under the glowing seaweed
shimmering glistens beneath

energy of a new me.

Return to living in simplicity
surrender to natures seasons
in your oceans you will swim deeply
not cursed
just an open heart
that feels the thirst of humanity
gasping for love to breathe blue light
she lands back in tonight.
A balance of it all
you see
mountains ripple open
heavenly purple is painted high
no wisp in sight to hold her back from embodying her light
that has always been a constant echo
of love
pulsing through open
s p a c e s

music tip-toes

my head follows the beat
voice speaks
openly
the words I receive come from the divine cosmic energy
letters crumble into this stream
tumbling speeds of light filter through the grey and the blue
the veil is too thin to ignore the truth
welcome in the epiphanies

Where you are meant to be is found beneath your feet.

I am today
who I will never be again
the sun will rise
and I may wear the same skin
yet a fresh canvas
welcomes me to my own painting
I remember I orchestrate my days with
the colours of my mind
cleansed in day light
I choose to find the rainbow delights
and incarnate into my own
pot of gold
I nourish my soil
with Mother Earths tweeting grace
I find solace in my forever becoming.

Live outside of time

observe what closes you to see what opens you

don't search for the safety net
it can only catch you if you release your grip

unwind your own fingertips into the ethereal moments
that create life

let go of the things you don't know.

You are an island in the ocean of my mind.

Do not be afraid of the path you are walking
perhaps the steps aren't fully paved and you
can't see beyond the cobble stones,
this is okay
lean into trusting yourself

 one breath at a time
 one step at a time
 one thing at a time.

You are deserving of all that is destined for you
trust in the seeds you are growing
water them
nurture them

the seeds you have planted know exactly how and when to sprout
all that is asked of you is patience and love.

-You wouldn't tell a flower to hurry its growth
for you know that the flower instinctively knows it is growing
in perfect timing,
apply this to your own seeds
don't rush the process
be gentle
be kind
be soft.

Recalibration of my cells
birds sing
they are my favourite hymn
I indulge in
to my nest of linen

holding Ted a little closer tonight
he lets out a sigh
his paws rest in my palms
I clasp onto his sentient life
this isn't a poem
I'm just grateful to be alive

for it's the little things
that are actually the big things
the moments that go unnoticed
are the memories we hold dear and close.

Soaking in water
exhaling my grip
to the tidal wave I find myself surrendering within
swimming through worlds underwater
I meet myself anew
same skin
yet not familiar
a walk in
to a body I didn't know was mine to nurture
a walk in
to a mind full of unanswered trauma
terrors held under water.

I breathed Sophie into the dust as Rose began to bloom.

As She Falls, She Rises

I came back to life unwillingly at first
until a feather imprinted upon my skin shook me into my freedom
now fully devoted to reminding the souls that are still asleep
to return to their intuition

working for the ones addicted to the medias feeding

but what about the seven hundred million still starving?
It's a viscious cycle
off balence like a penny farthing

I won't conform to the standards of a worldwide cult
worshiping the inhumane
insane
deep state

standing in a crowded line as one by one they attempt to train and chain
using scare tactics as bate.

Do you see the purpose in your being?

Your life is supposed to be fully lived

your breath deeply breathed

your eyes entirely seen

your soul energetically gleaming

you are intended to live with your heart wide open

your vessel is an extension of you as it is you

your dermis is a home for the beating drum within

yout iris resembles worlds that only you can dream in

you are here to be seen

your body is thriving

trust the voice that speaks softly

you are loved

so

dearly.